A Smile in My Heart

A Gentle story of Holding Grandpa Close, Even When He's Gone

"For every little heart learning
to say goodbye—
may you always feel the smile
of love in your heart
that never goes away."

This Book Belongs to

_____

Copyright

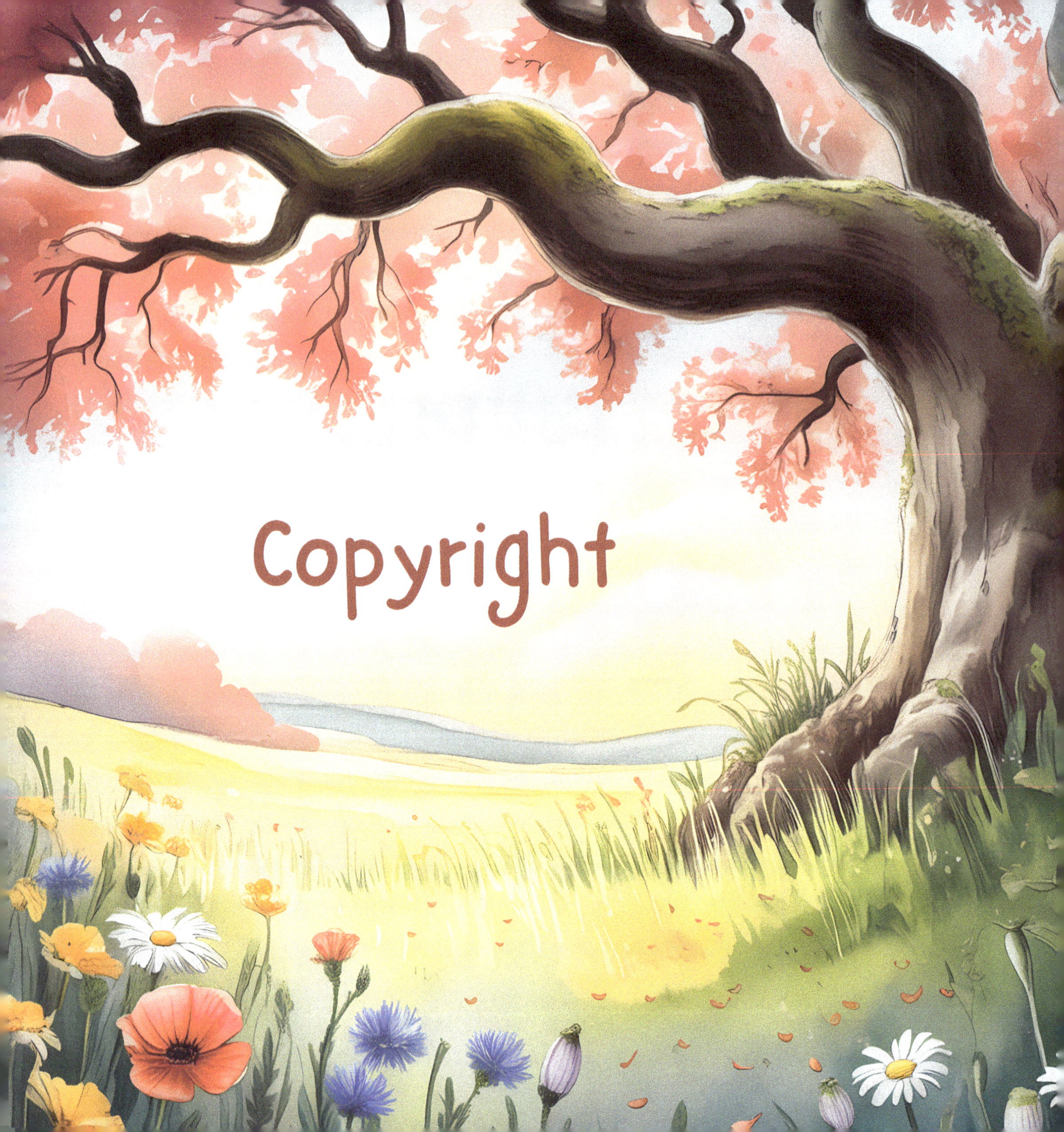

Book Cover by Tukotuku Publishing

Illustrations by Tukotuku Publishing

First edition 2025

Print ISBN:978-1-991366-25-2

Ebook ISBN:978-1-991366-26-9

Hi there, little one

This is a story about missing someone very special—like a Grandpa—
and learning that even when someone is gone, their love can still
stay with us. Sometimes our hearts feel big and stormy,
and that's okay.
This book is here to help you feel safe, warm, and loved while you
remember the happy times.
Let's take a gentle journey together.
Love,
Michelle

Written with Empathy and Care

this story reminds families that saying goodbye doesn't mean forgetting... It means remembering with love.

My Grandfather Isn't Here Anymore

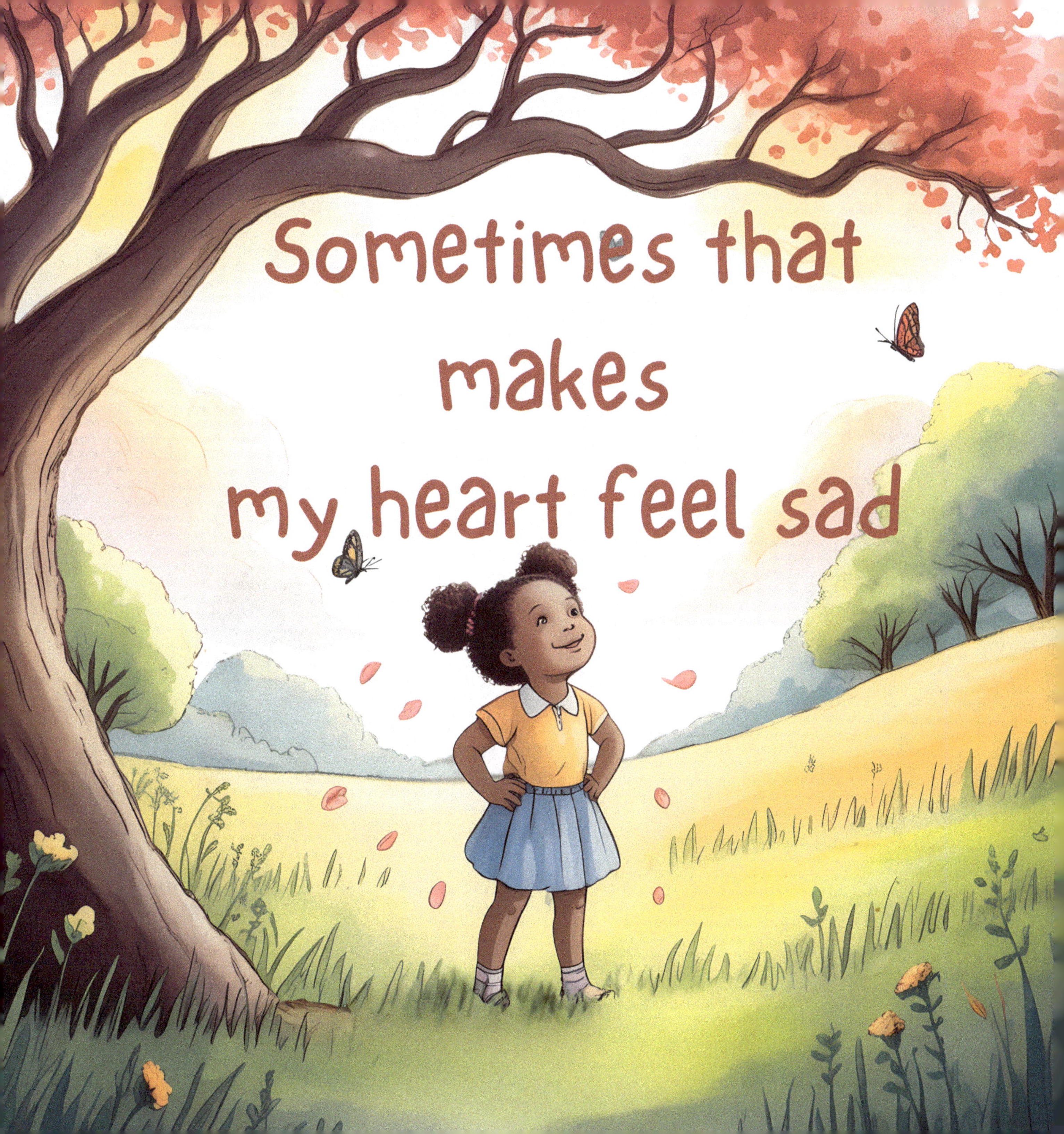

Sometimes that makes my heart feel sad

It Feels Big and Stormy Inside,

like a rainy day

that's called
Grief

Grief
means
I love him a lot...

And I miss
him just as much.

Sometimes I Cry

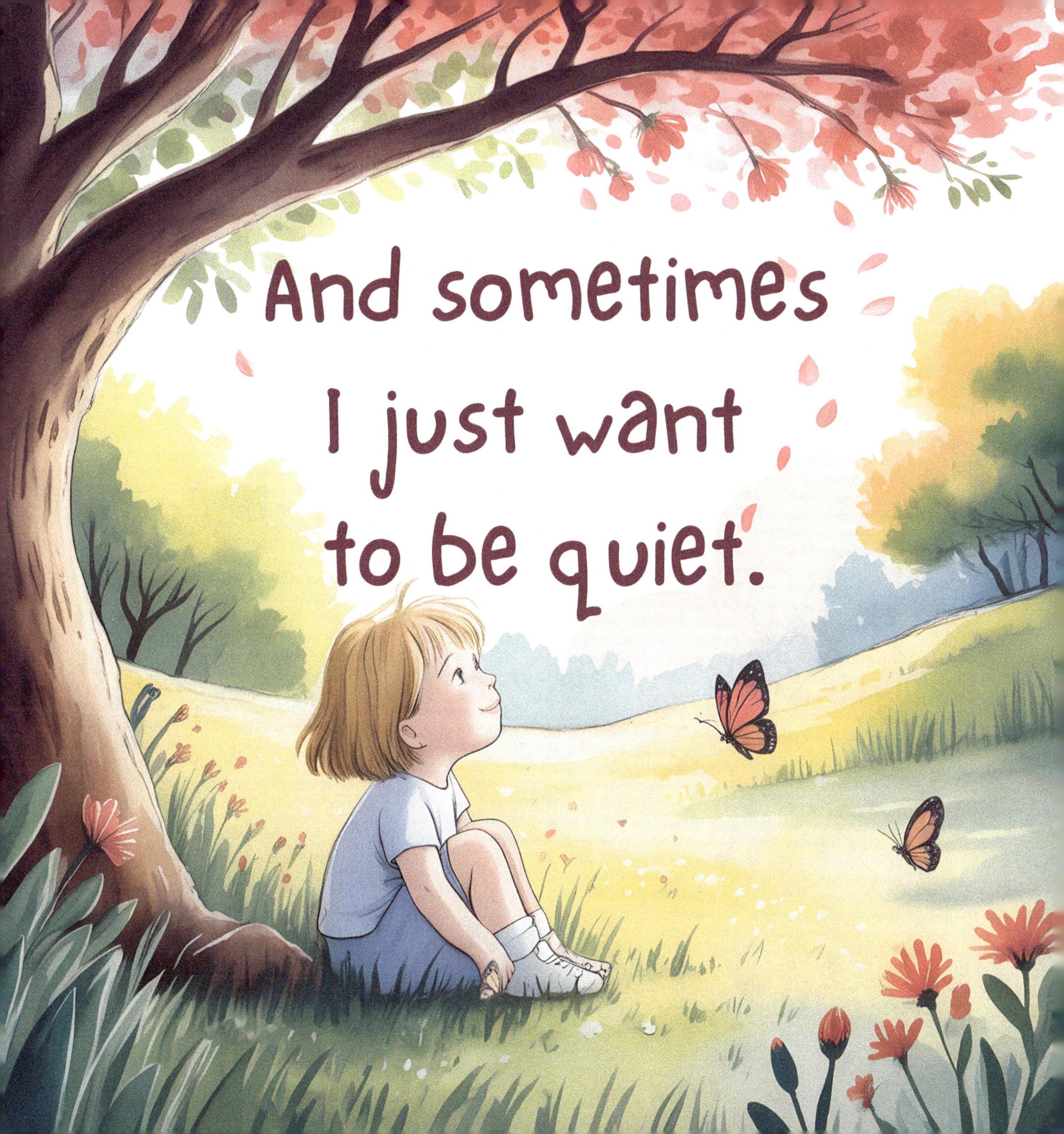

And sometimes I just want to be quiet.

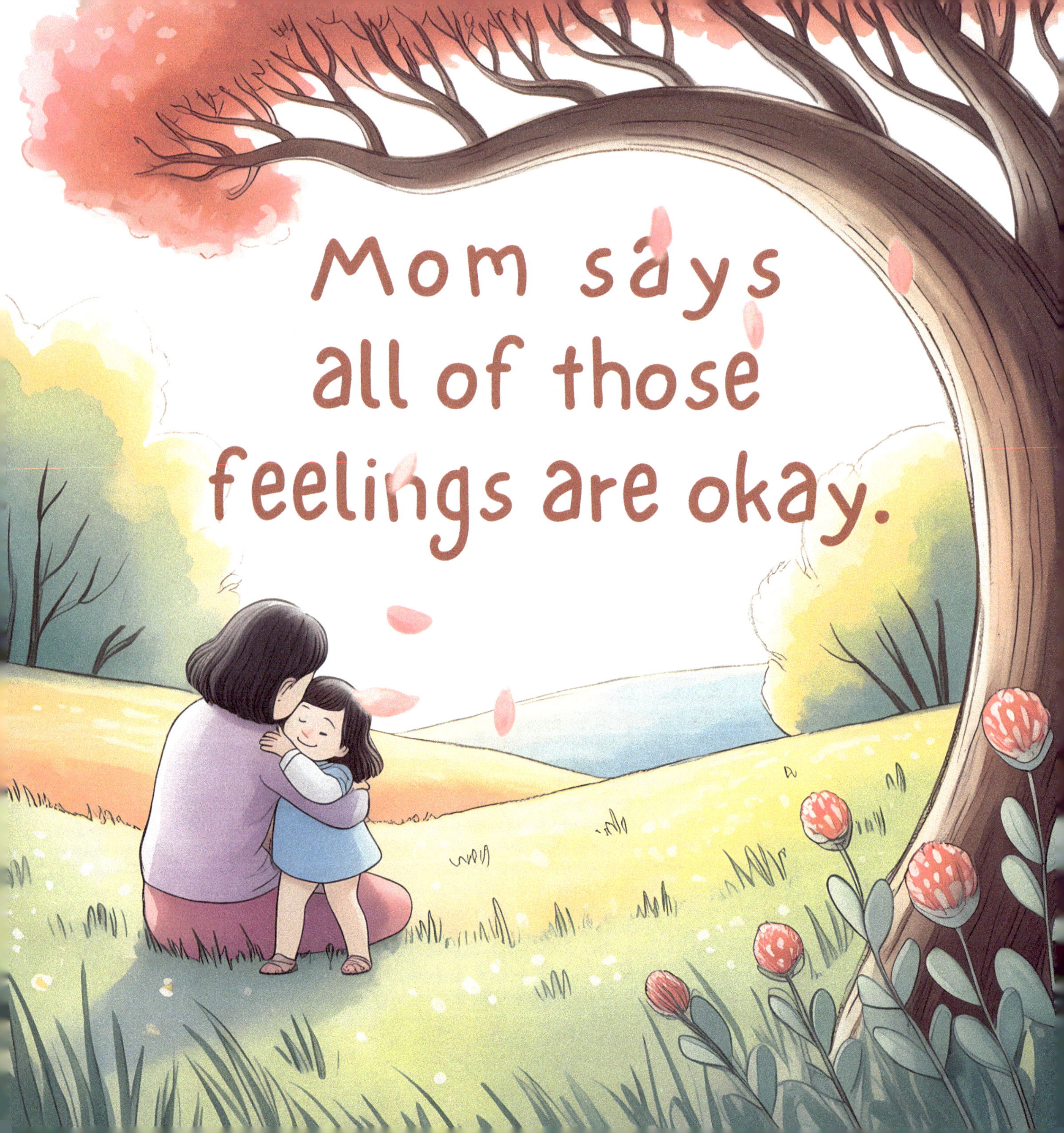

Mom says all of those feelings are okay.

She cuddles me close
when I feel
sad and wobbly.

I Remember Grandpa's Hands

they were
warm and
strong

I Remember His Laugh

It made my whole tummy giggle

We Did Everything Together

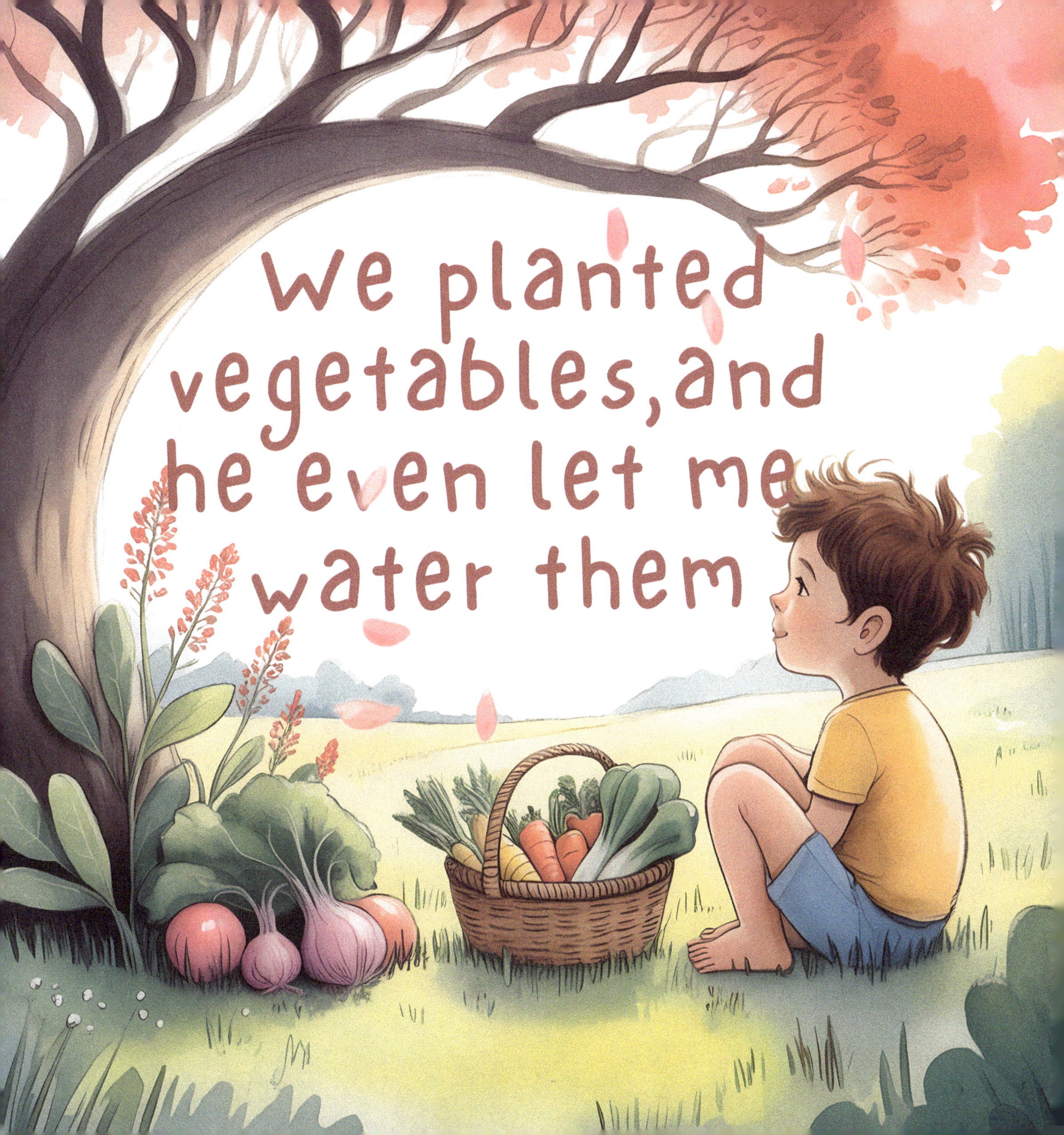

We planted vegetables, and he even let me water them

Now, I Plant Flowers Just or Him

And they grow
with love,
and Sunshine

Sometimes, I Write Letters to Koro

And I tell him
what I've been
up to

I DRAW
PICTURES
TOO

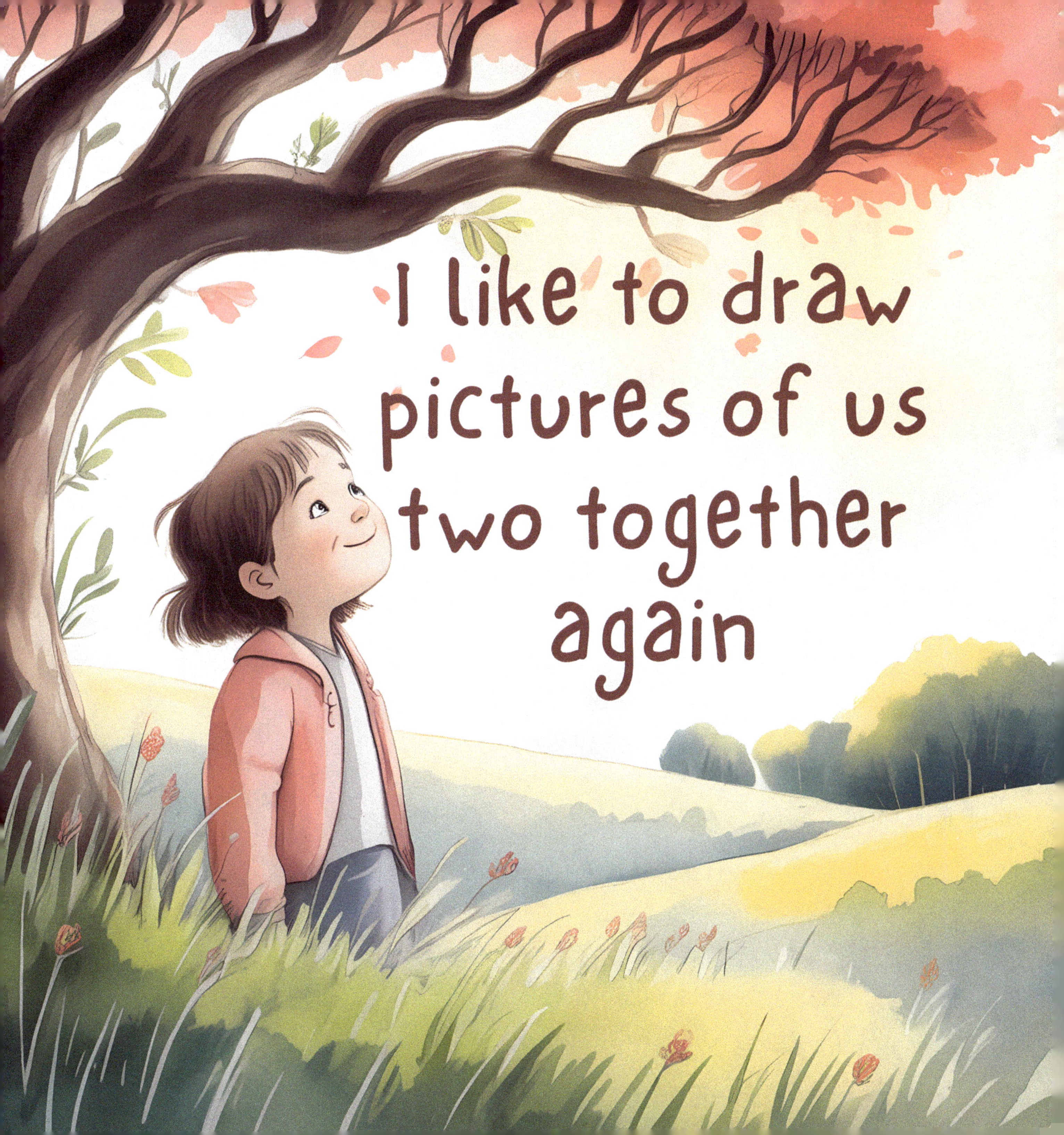

I like to draw pictures of us two together again

And then yesterday

I had a thought
I decided to make a

Memory Box

And I filled
it with
everything that
reminded
me of him

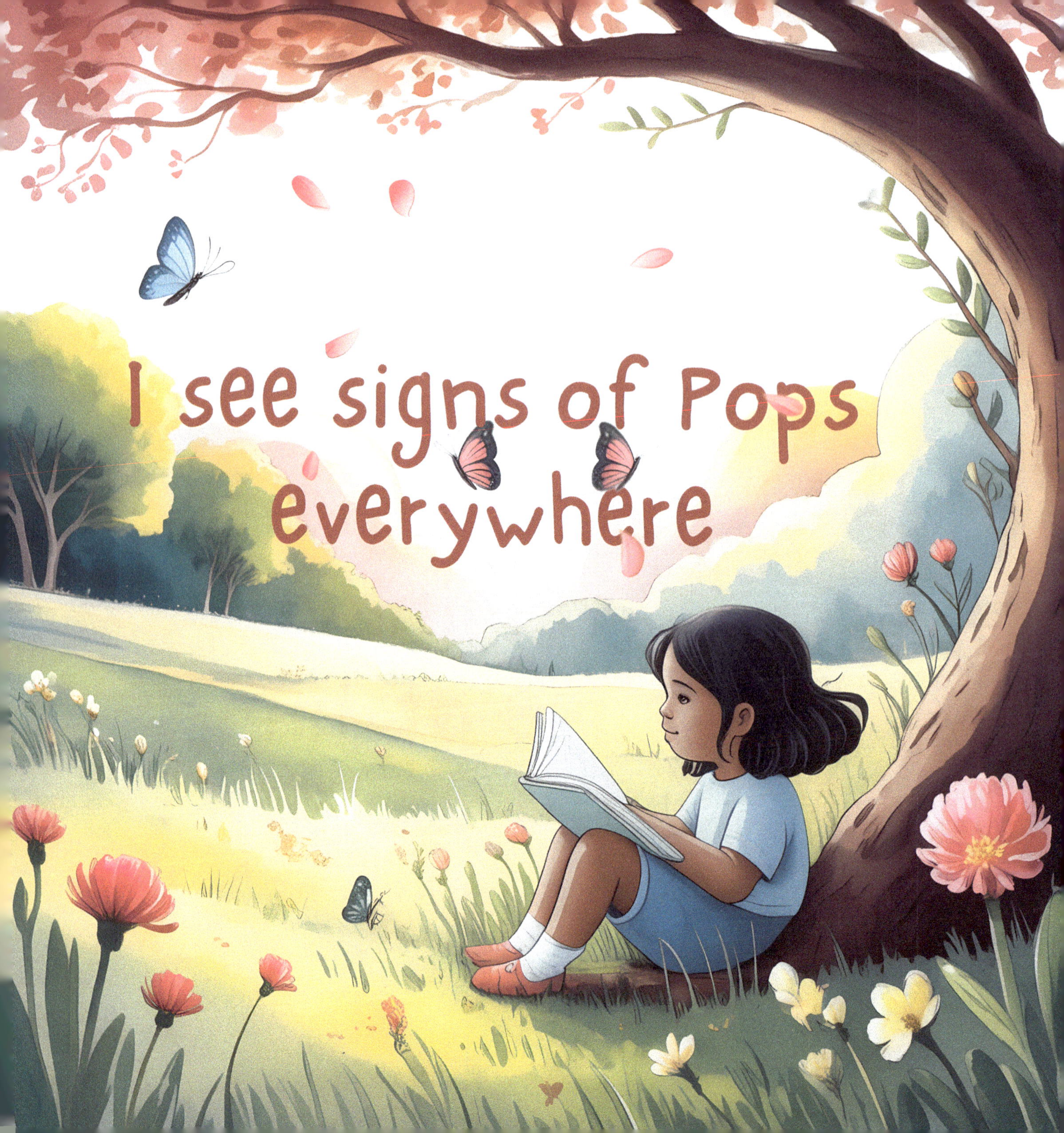

I see signs of Pops everywhere

In the butterflies, in the clouds, in the flower's and trees and in the stories that he told.

Even though Grandpa is Gone....

His love
is still here

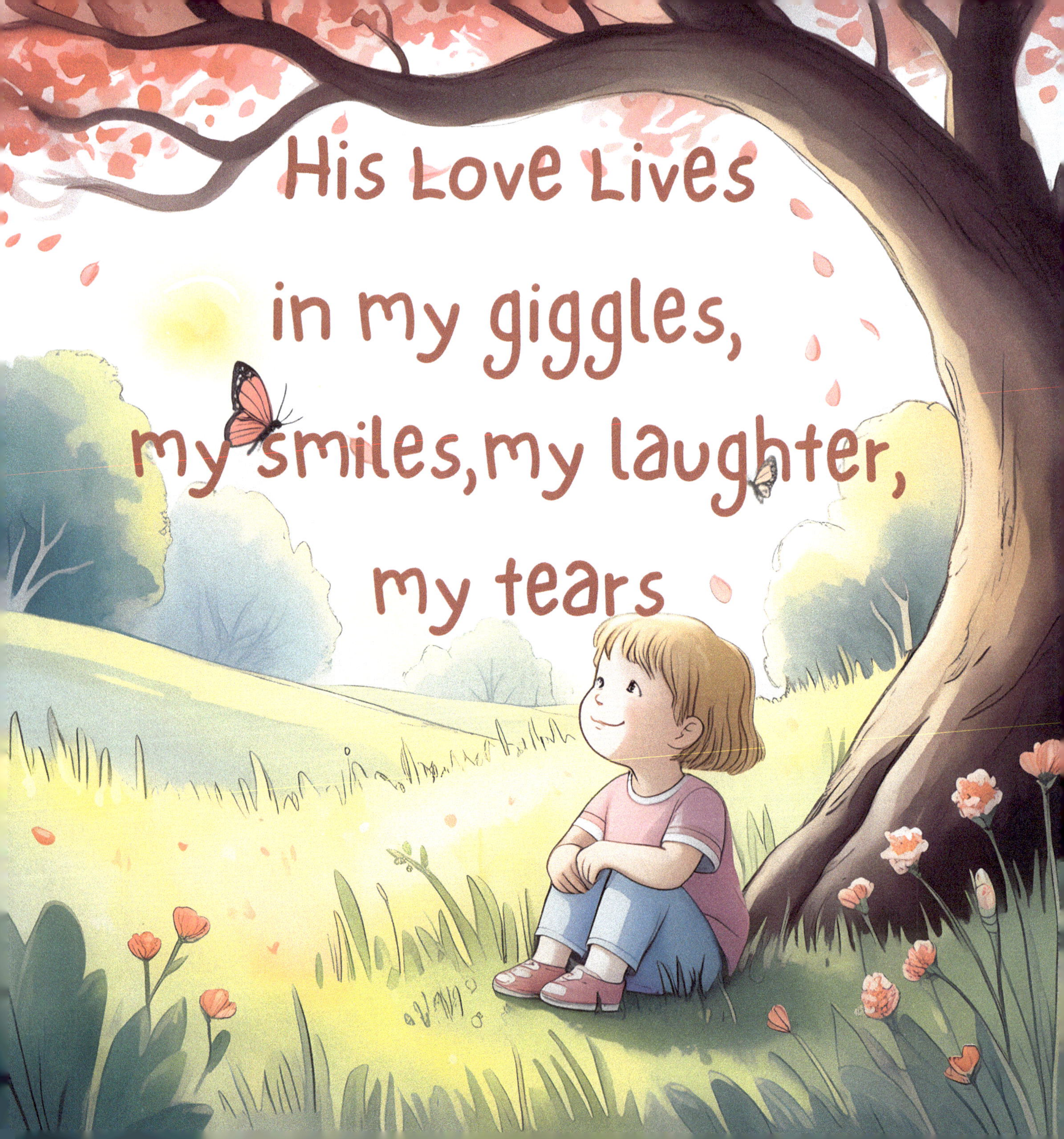

His Love Lives

in my giggles,

my smiles,my laughter,

my tears

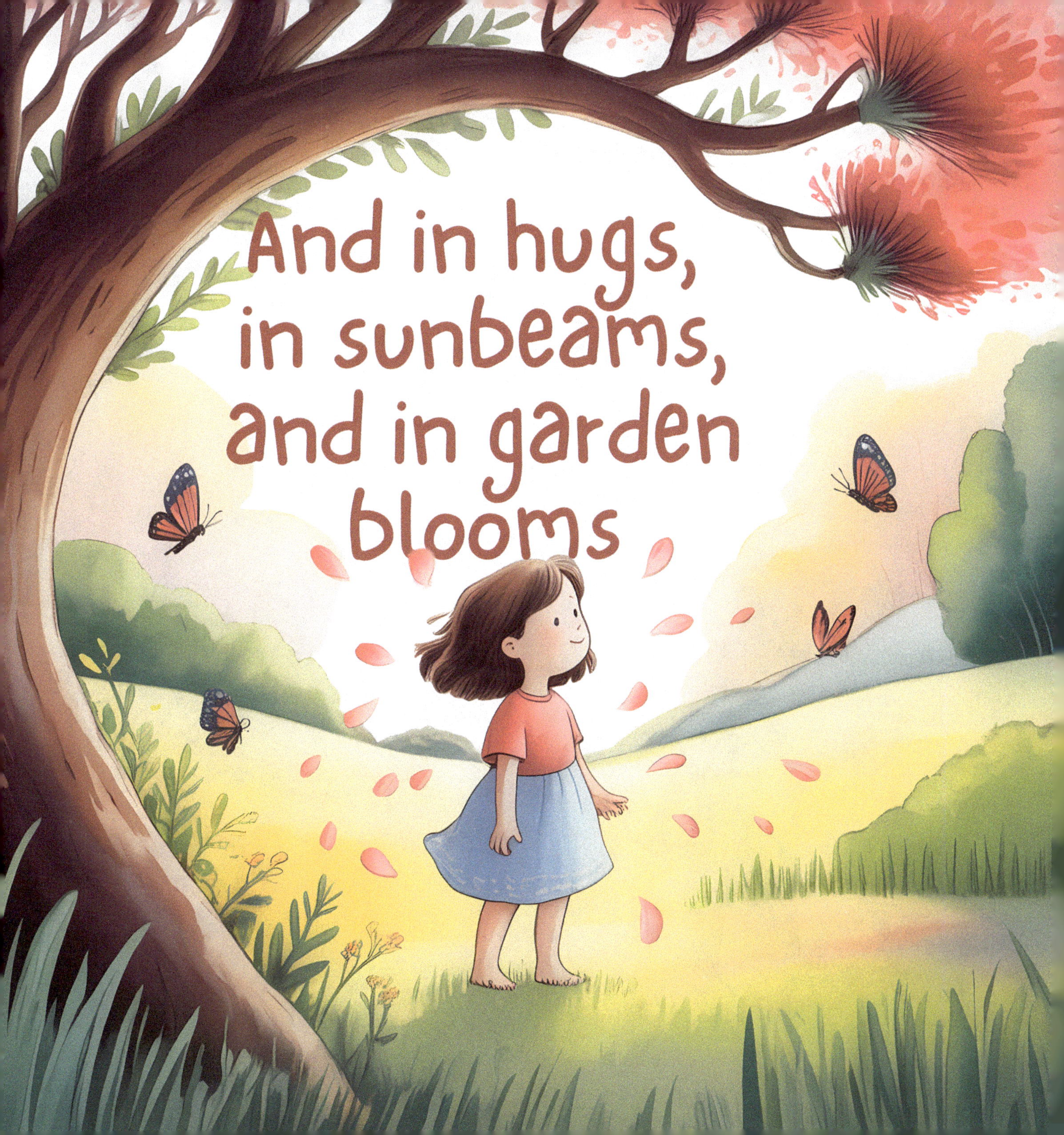

And in hugs,
in sunbeams,
and in garden
blooms

Some Days
I Feel Sad.

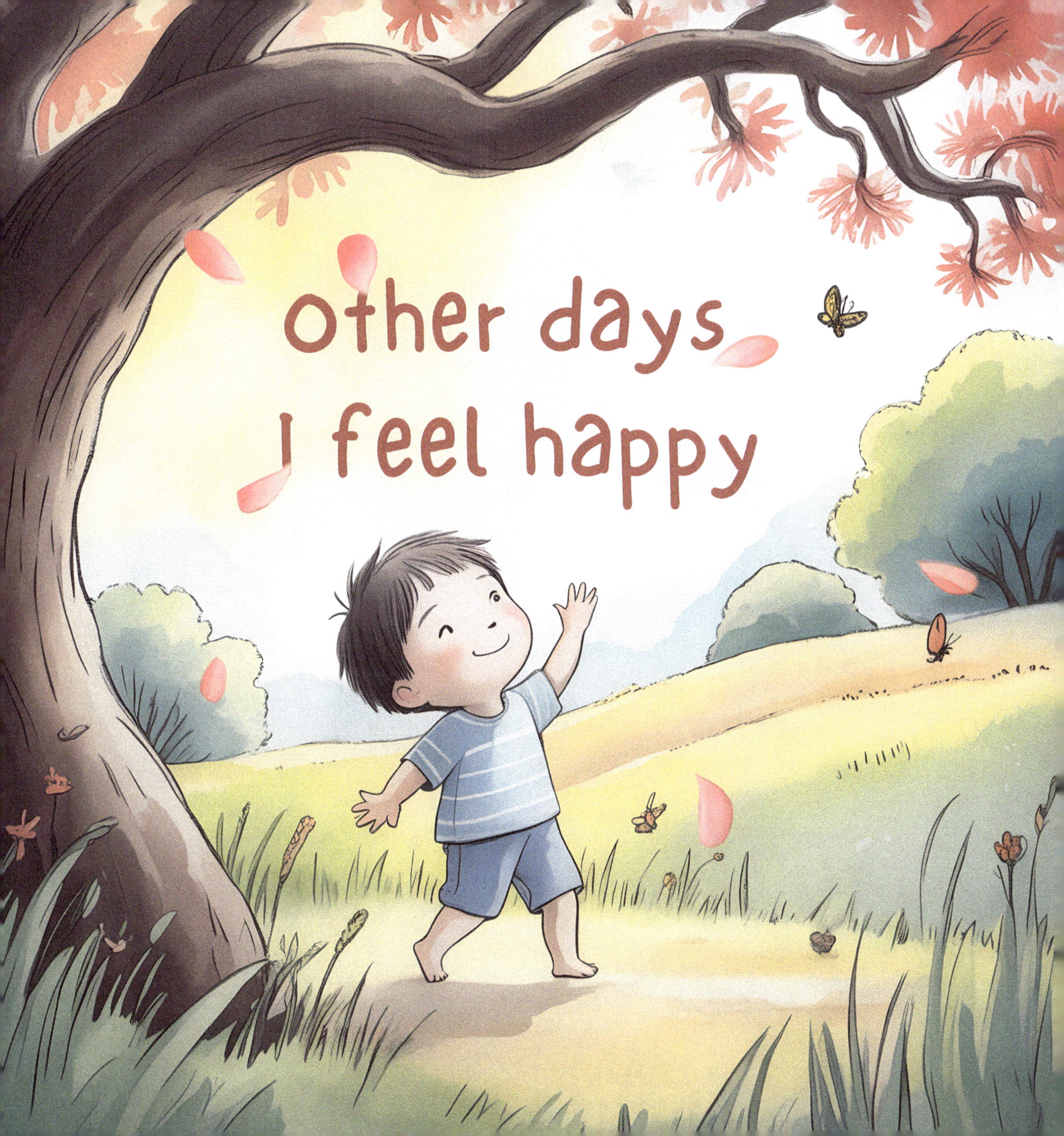

other days
I feel happy

And Every Day...

I carry a smile
in my heart
just for Gramps

Because Love
Never really Leaves

It
just
changes shape

And even when
someone is gone,
their Love will always
stay Close,
it becomes a smile in our
heart

Forever
and
Always

Let's
Write a Note
to Grandpa

Can you draw a Picture of Pops?

Why not Draw A Favorite Memory that you have with Koro

What would
you like
to tell Nonno?

Draw something
that made your
Grampy
different and unique

Draw a memory that makes you smile when you think of Papa

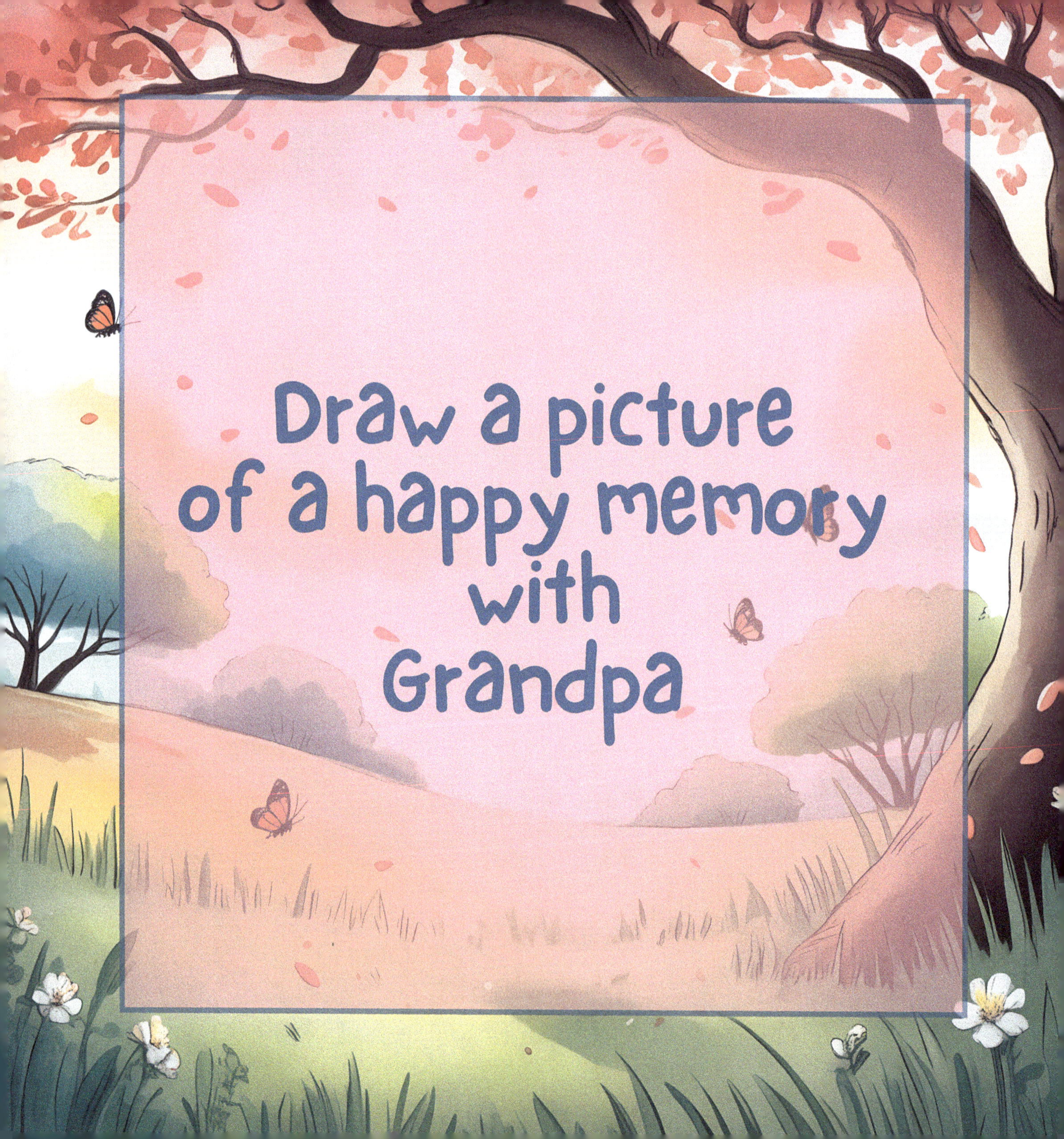
Draw a picture of a happy memory with Grandpa

Let's create your own story about Grandpop. It can be happy, sad, funny, or all of those. Start with "Once upoun A time...."

A Note for your Heart

When someone you love – like a Grandfather leaves you,
it can feel like your heart has a missing piece.
But little by little, as you remember the cuddles,
the playtimes, and the love you shared...
something amazing happens.
that missing piece becomes a memory,
and that memory becomes part of who you are.
Your heart grows.
And the love you gave –
and felt –
stays with you, always.
Wherever you go,
whatever you do,
your Grandfather's Smile
will walk beside you...
tucked safely in your heart.

THE END

A Note
for grown-ups

Supporting your Child through the loss of a Grandfather

Losing a grandparent is often a child's first experience with deep grief. It can bring up big feelings—sadness, confusion, even fear. A Smile in My Heart was created to gently help your child explore those emotions and begin the healing journey through love,
memories, and creativity.
Here's how you can support them along the way:
Let them talk freely about Grandpa and what they miss.
Encourage drawing, storytelling,
or letter writing to express feelings.
Reassure them that all emotions are okay—
there's no wrong way to grieve.
Share your own memories and feelings, showing that it's okay to feel and remember together.
This book is a soft space where your child can feel safe, loved, and reminded that even though Gramps is gone, his love still lives in their heart.

Validate
their Feelings

Children may express sadness, anger,
guilt, or even relief.
All of these are normal.
Let your child know it's okay to feel
what they're feeling — and that grief
doesn't have a timeline.
Say things like-

**"I miss Koro too." Let
your child know it's okay to
feel sad.
"I'm here for you."**

Create Space
for Expression

Encourage creative outlets-drawing,

journaling,storytelling.
or even role-playing.
Let them choose how they'd like to honor
and remember their pops.

Talk Honestly About Death

Use age appropriate language Avoid confusing phrases like "went to sleep" — instead, gently explain that all living beings have a life cycle. Honest conversations build trust and emotional resilience.

Rituals
Can Help

Creating a memory box,
planting a flower,
or holding a simple ceremony
can give children
a sense of closure and a tangible
way to say goodbye.

Model Healthy Grieving

If you're grieving it's okay to show it. When children see you sharing your emotions openly, it reasures them that sadness is part of love — not something to hide..

Most importantly,
Their Grandfather may be gone,
but the bond they shared will always be part
of who they are.

with love,

Michelle

This Book is part of a gentle
grief series called
"Hearts that Remember" and is
for little ones who are learning
to love, lose,
and remember

"Let's meet
Michelle Huirama"

Hi! I'm Michelle, and I write gentle picture books for little ones learning about big feelings. When my own loved ones passed away, I wished there had been a soft, simple story I could read to the children in my life—something that would help them feel safe, loved, and less alone. That's why I wrote A Smile in My Heart. It's a gentle hug in book form, made to help children understand grief and remember the love that never goes away. I believe even the smallest hearts deserve stories that bring light during dark times. I hope this book brings comfort to your family and helps keep Grandpa's love shining bright.

Ko Tukotuku te Reikura
Ko Tamainupo te Hapu
Ko Karioi te Maunga
Ko Waikato te Ipukarea
Ko Tainui te Waka

More
Books

From Michelle Huirama

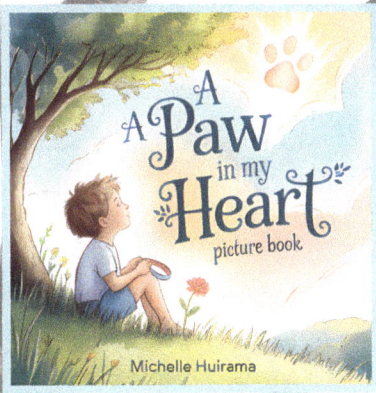

A
A **Paw**
in my
Heart
picture book

Michelle Huirama

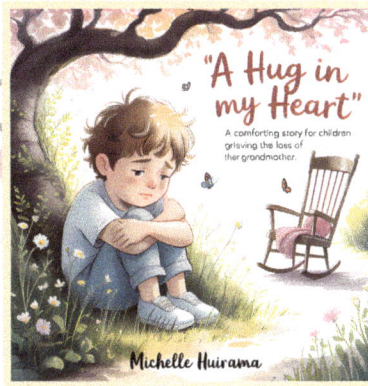

"A Hug in
my Heart"

A comforting story for children
grieving the loss of
their grandmother.

Michelle Huirama

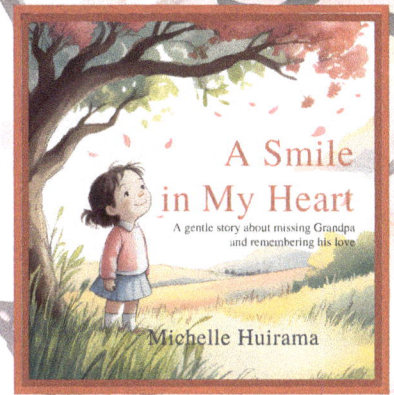

A Smile
in My Heart

A gentle story about missing Grandpa
and remembering his love

Michelle Huirama

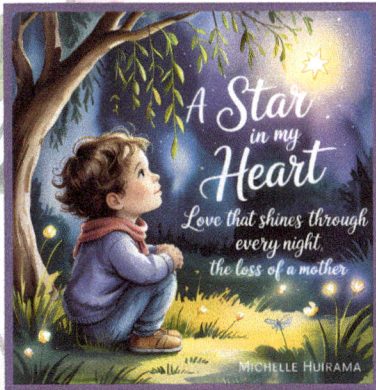

A *Star*
in my
Heart

*Love that shines through
every night,
the loss of a mother*

MICHELLE HUIRAMA

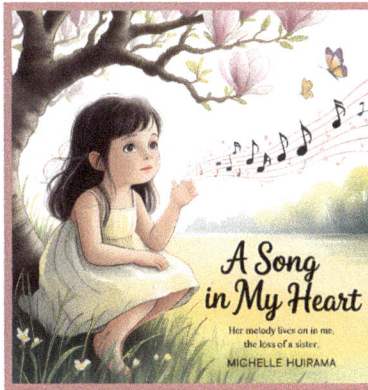

A Song
in My Heart

Her melody lives on in me,
the loss of a sister,
MICHELLE HUIRAMA

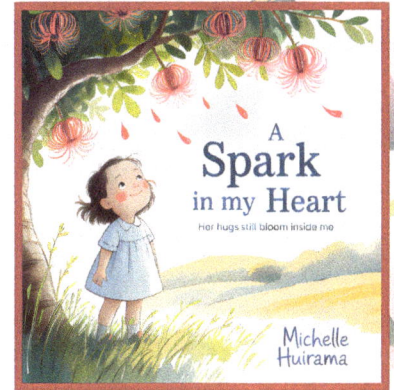

A
Spark
in my **Heart**

Her hugs still bloom inside me

Michelle
Huirama

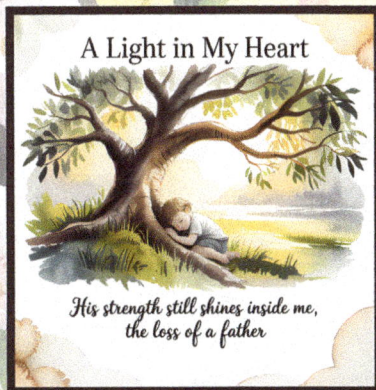

A Light in My Heart

*His strength still shines inside me,
the loss of a father*

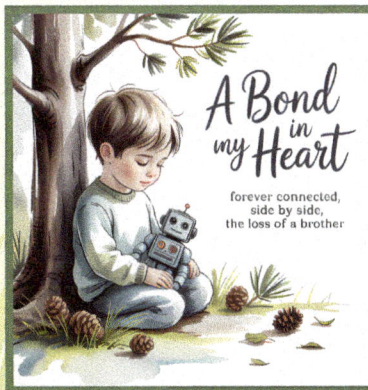

A Bond
in
my Heart

forever connected,
side by side,
the loss of a brother

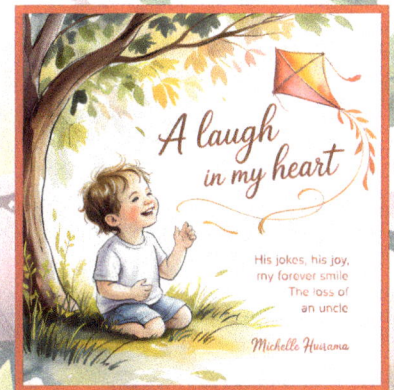

A laugh
in my heart

His jokes, his joy,
my forever smile
The loss of
an uncle

Michelle Huirama

www.ingramcontent.com/pod-product-compliance
Lightning Source LLC
Chambersburg PA
CBHW080522090426
42734CB00015B/3133